With the Eyes
of a
RAPTOR

Other works by
E. A. Mares
include:

The Unicorn Poem

The Unicorn Poem & Flowers and Songs of Sorrow

There Are Four Wounds, Miguel

*I Returned and Saw Under the Sun:
Padre Martínez of Taos*

With the Eyes of a RAPTOR

selected poems by

E. A. Mares

San Antonio, Texas
2004

With the Eyes of a Raptor © 2004
by E. A. Mares

Cover illustration © 2004 by Vered Mares

First Edition

ISBN: 0-930324-58-7 (paperback)

Wings Press
627 E. Guenther
San Antonio, Texas 78210
Phone/fax: (210) 271-7805

On-line catalogue and ordering:
www.wingspress.com

Cataloging In Publication Data:

Mares, Ernesto A.
    With the Eyes of a Raptor / E. A. Mares.

                130 p. ; 14 cm.
ISBN 0-930324-58-7 (pbk.)

1.Poetry. 2. Literature—Latino 3. Literature—Southwest I.
Title.

Library of Congress Control Number:
2004100893

For Carolyn, Maria, Vered,
Ernesto . . . and always Galit

Table of contents

I. In the Taverna Onanas

II. There Are Four Wounds, Miguel

III. In My Violin Dream

IV. With the Eyes of a Raptor

V. The Discourse of Little Dog and Big Dog

I.

In the
Taverna Ononas

Aphrodite Hotel, The Placa

Athens, 5:30 a.m.

Birdsong weaves a splash of dark roofs,
whitewashed walls, and green awnings
into a cool dawn of gray hills
south from the fifth floor window.

The Parthenon rises to the west renewed
by sunlight and the singing of swallows.
Nearby, a Greek Orthodox Temple
In a cubist surround of buildings

lifts its cross to the milky sky.
Beneath the cupola of battered red tiles,
maroon flowers wildly cascade
down the brick walls. Revving up,

a car annoys the sleeping city.
White laundry on a distant balcony
catches the sun, flutters the day.

Athens, The Agora

Near the ruins a few dogs
and sickly cats hang around the tavernas.
Tourists, no longer wearing togas,
stroll like conquerors.
After all, the empire fares well.

X number of bombs = Y number of days
to solve the equation of Balkan wars.
The global economy has green hair,
silicone breasts, and ATM machines.
Internet stock soars like Chinese rockets.

Still, the Greek Zapatistas scribble
"we demand our own dreams"
on the remnants of walls shadowed
by almond, myrtle, and pomegranate.

Tourists heavy with Aegean food
survey the Parthenon, walk through
old Hadrian's arch. They don't notice
Socrates and his friends hanging out
in the Agora, debating something.

They see nothing. Not the philosophers,
not the feral dogs, cold-eyed and hungry.
They pant. Their ribs show. They wait.

Goats Near Delphi

In Apollo's Temple
I think the Oracle at Delphi
is silent. Later, down the mountain
I hear the goats, their soft calls
to each other, and their bells
murmuring like the voices
of poets on Mount Parnassus.

The goats descend the steep trail
to the Sacred Plain and the sea
beyond the Bay of Itea. I still hear
their bells, the poets' songs,
sailing out to the world. The wind
at my back carries the music,
the Oracle's voice, through the trees.

Oedipus

Surely he looked down from Delphi
to Hrisso and then to the port city,
Itea. He remarked to himself
upon the vast orchestral work
of mountain, sea, and sky.

He thought of the long walk
past the Triple Way back to Thebes.
There would be the tavernas,
table wine and food.
And he had a good story
for the travelers. He had solved
the riddle of the sphinx.

He knew nothing of Freud,
the long shadow cast back to his father.
Nothing of the fight to come.
The dead king. The older, enticing, widow.

No, he only saw Hrissos and Itea
from the heights of Delphi.
He didn't recognize the setting
for a story of patricide, incest,
and blindness. No, he daydreamed,
hypnotized by the sweep of the land.

So he missed his step, didn't even see
the old man, the raised whip, and Homer
off in the shadows. Oedipus didn't know
he had stumbled into our world.

Tyrens

The Cyclops built these walls.
Massive stone blocks
no man could have moved
shimmer in the sun.
Homer sang of these stones.

Between the jagged shards,
red poppies grow.
They remember the Cyclops,
Homer, the song.

Moon Over Andros Beach

in memory of Galit

Tonight the blacksmith moon hammers
a plating of silver on the Aegean Sea.

From the town of Chora, above, a halo
dim as candlelight spreads over the beach.

Daughter, your voice comes ashore,
lingers in the pools of liquid moonlight

left behind by the sea's ebb. The waves
bring you back again and again.

The ceaseless churning and tumbling
of pebbles, history, and memory.

Mira La Luna

This land of the Hellenes rises
like Tenochtitlán, the ruins
of Teotihuacan and the Mexican moon.

Here Poseidon threw down his trident.
Athena planted her olive tree and claimed
the Acropolis. The gods favored her.

Athena's moon is of olives and wine,
La Placa moon, taverna moon,
la llorona moon, gravestone moon.

"Mira la luna," I said to my daughter.
It is still her moon. Forever.

In The Taverna Ononas

The raven-eyed young woman
serves filet of fresh monkfish.
She says "meet the fisherman."
Her father, a rugged and tan fifties,
waves, asks if the fish is good.
"Very good. It is very good,"
I say in broken Greek.
He is retired navy, speaks Spanish.
Freed from linguistic hell, I ask
"¿Por qué se llama la taverna Ononas?"
"Mi abuelo. Él pescaba aquí," he says.

Tonight the omicron moon, olive oil moon,
rises over Andros Bay, over the Aegean,
rises like fresh fish, garlic, and wine,
rises like Ononas from long ago.

Same Old Song

I heard a Greek say:
"We never had to lock our doors.
It's because of the Albanians."

Another Greek said:
"The Americans pay the Albanians
five thousand dollars to fight.
The Albanians aren't good fighters."

One more Greek said:
"We have a terrible problem.
The Albanians steal everything."

I heard a Greek poet say:
 "The stranger and the enemy,
we have seen him in the mirror."*

He knew his Greeks and his Albanians.
He knew you. He knew me.

* *George Seferis*

Rudy

Rudy is the next door neighbor's dog.
He understands only Greek. No Spanish,
no English. His eyes speak the language of Wags,
the language of Lassie, of Tycho, of Relámpago,
and Mokey, of Sukie, of Chicarrón, the dogs
of one name, of no history, of an eternal now.

Rudy looks at me with the marble stare
of Praxiteles' Hermes in the Andros Museum,
and the blank stare of the nameless dog
who followed me from Andros to Livadia.

I threw rocks at him to turn him back.
So he wouldn't get lost. The trouble is
we were friends already. I encouraged him
to follow me, punished him for doing so.

Bad to throw rocks. Worse for him to get lost.
Rudy, stay well. Stay home. Bark at the moon.
Forgive me for being inept with your kin.

The Song in the Mexican Cantina

(after Odysseus Elytis)

Here where the sun washes the courtyards
at dawn and glistens in the arched rock,
do I hear the song from the Mexican cantina
in Morelia carried here by the waves?
Guitars and trumpets for the Aegean Sea?
Is it the song in the Mexican cantina exciting
the swallows into flight? Chattering as they dart
among the palm trees and rocks below?

When the firm-breasted girl claws the back
of her lover at the faint glow of morning,
tell me, is it the song of mariachis
come drifting across oceans, through olive trees
to turn back the coverlet, guiding
their arms in the omicron motions of love?

High on the Pyramid at Teotihuacan
every day is an offering to the sun.
Is it the song in the cantina there
lilting down the Valley of Anahuac,
echoing through all the seas of the world?
Tell me, is it the song, the Mexican song,
women sway to in the streets of Andros town?

The fisherman waves his arm as we dine
in the taverna called Ononas.
Tell me, is it the song in the Mexican cantina
cooling our brows with canciones across
cold waves, fire sun, and the moon's rigging?

From beyond the horizon and the sea, tell me,
does the Mexican song charm the solar wind,
spawn the weather front where the mountain drops
into Andros Bay? Tell me, is it the song
in the Mexican cantina far down the beach
bringing me violins, trumpets, and guitars?

While tourists from the empire stride the cool
beach of April or the oven streets
of August, and the moon slaps its heel,
do you hear a girl sigh in the caves below
the marble cliff? Do you hear the guitarrón
strum the stars to glimmer in the night?
Tell me, is it the song in the Mexican cantina?

One Greek Spoon and a 'Fridgerator Magnet

(for 'la güera' at the Barelas Coffee Shop)

I bring back to "Burque"
a 'fridgerator magnet and
one Greek spoon from Athens

'La Güera' of Barelas Coffee Shop fame
would like to sip chocolate in the Greek dawn
stir her coffee near Syntagma Square

She opens the 'fridgerator door and
sees the Parthenon on the magnet
orange juice and skim milk
taste better with classical thoughts

Somewhere inside she feels her lips
pucker up to Homer and Plato
to Greek metrics and golden numbers

Wingless Victory rises from the magnet
shapes 'la güera' into a pale caryatid
dancing Barelas Coffee Shop trays

II.

There are
Four Wounds, Miguel

Con tres heridas yo:
la de la vida,
la del amor,
la de la muerte.

I come with three wounds:
the wound of life,
the wound of love,
the wound of death.

– Miguel Hernandez
E.A. Mares, translator

There Are Four Wounds, Miguel

The sand hill cranes rise, wheel
and turn above the Rio Grande. Their wings
flash in the sun and their wavering V
floats north and then is gone.
There is a fourth wound, Miguel,
the silence these birds leave in their wake.

The tree house in my father's cottonwood
warps into something like a photograph
left too long in the sun,
all children having grown and gone.
There is a fourth wound, Miguel,
the silence of the tree house planks.

Once I saw a guitar burnt and blackened by fire.
The strings were gone, the bridge destroyed,
the neck and body only dark shadows.
There is a fourth wound, Miguel,
a silence where once there was music.

One by one the days slip into history,
and where there was a voice
there are only documents, evidence
that my daughter once walked this land.
Now she leaves footprints only in memory.

There are four wounds, Miguel,
the wound of life,
the wound of love,
the wound of death,
the wound of silence.

Bat Mitzvah: May 1, 1986

You come of age, Galit,
and you speak about the stunted tree
with no roots save only in human things.

There is the good tree, you say,
with roots in the deep waters,
the rich soil of your ancient religion.

Even during the ceremony, Galit,
I hope your words will hold you
to a good place inside yourself.

When it's my turn to speak,
I follow your metaphor of the tree
and I see crystalline leaves

fluttering like wings inside your imagination,
that luminous and fragile beauty.
I fear for you, my lovely daughter.

I mean to say we are all stunted trees,
that only love holds the leaves
when the great winds of failure strike.

Soon, the dead leaves swirl away,
the stunted tree falls
and the promise of seed waits for next spring.

I mean to say all humans fail
and that failing together we shall rise
at last on wide and clamorous wings

like a flock of sand hill cranes. We'll form
a victorious V against the sun.
We will fly together, daughter.

I still mean to say that.

The Flight

First the frantic calls.
Some fierce duende crackling over the lines:
"your daughter . . . the hospital . . . hurry . . ."
Then the fast packing of clothes, books . . .
what to take . . . will she make it . . . what if . . .
All questions take flight on silent wings.

Speechless, my wife drives me to DFW.
There I sit and recall the photographs,
Scene after scene of my daughter's life.
The color turns to sepia tone and is gone.
Surely she will be there waiting, I think.

She will rally, surely, as so many times before.
I remember that time in middle school,
she was ten, growing fast, and we played our game:
running towards me she would leap into my arms,
but the last time I embraced her too late, dropped her,
scared us both and we never played that way again.
Now I want nothing more than to never drop my child.

I take my usual window seat.
No one speaks to me. The passengers sense
A mythic bird has settled on my shoulders
and wrapped its dark wings around me like a shroud.
At the runway's edge a surge of power
brings the plane to life. I hope high tech
will not fail her now.

The Super 80 banks sharply to the west,
cuts through a thin cloud and flies above fields
as they come into view, then vanish, like chapters
in a history no one understands.
I am flying home to my daughter.

The Hospital

She was born here twenty years ago.
The nursery is on the first floor,
near an exit so the parents
won't have far to go to take their child
out into the world.

Now she is on the fourth floor,
intensive care unit, close to the doctors,
the machines, the whole life-sustaining dance
around the bonfire of death.
Close to the sky above. Easy exit
when the dance ends, the rock concert
truly turned to stone.

She loved the hard-edged music,
Sid Vicious and Nancy. The Sex Pistols,
Metallica, Slayer, Iron Maiden,
the whole punk druggie scene.
She could scream with the best of them,
the surgical howl cutting her heart
away from all merely human contact.

Oh Galit, – Galit, Galit, Galite, Galit –
I rush to the fourth floor,
see the somber-faced nurse
and I know.
I see your mother's eyes
and I know.
I see the room marked No Admittance
and I know.
I see the sky filled with circling grackles and crows
and I know.
I have come too late to say goodbye to my daughter.

Oh, Galit – my old refrain from her childhood returns –
Galit, Galit, Galite, Galit.
You have taken my life with yours
and left me no place in this world.

She lies bathed in white neon light,
arms at her side, sheet up to her chin.
Four hours dead and cold to my touch.
Dark shadows ring her eyelids.

My army of words
cannot save the shattered country we share.
Behind my thin line of words,
my summing up of the facts,
chaos has taken the interior of the land.
There is rioting in my bloodstream,
anarchy in all my bones.

I try to retreat in good order,
down the elevator. Like Icarus
in the Brughel painting, I fall
into the city. No one hears the splash.
No one cares about my fall from grace.
The defeated country I have become.

Pásale

Pásale, canta Galit
desde el asiento trasero del carro.
Recuerda las palabras
del vendedor en Juárez
"Pásale, les va gustar."

Galit tiene dos años entonces.
Manejamos por la selva Gila
evadiendo la migra.
Pasamos de contrabando
a Otelia, linda mexicana,
que nos ayudará con la niña en casa.

Años después, agarran a Otelia
en la frontera.
Nunca jamás vamos a verla.
La primera pérdida de mi hija.
Desde entonces, Galit, agitada,
monta su caballito de madera
y casi nunca sonríe.

A veces sí que está contenta.
Yo le canto "pásale, mi 'jita."
Me sonríe con sus ojos olivos . . . musicales.

Llegan las guerras de adolescencia.
Los cambios feroces
de las células ardientes.
Las fotos revelan los ojos
que ya no cantan "pásale."
                    La música se vuelve
cada vez más chirriante,
                    áspera, metálica.

El movimiento final irracional
termina en el silencio.

Yo, que no creo en la religión burocrática,
        recuerdo mi hija
            mientras que ando meditando
en las orillas del río cuyos aguas
        llevan el invierno
            derritiéndose rumbo a México, al golfo.

Dentro de mi ser
        hay un lugar donde mi hija
                        baila como estas cigüeñas
haciendo piruetas hacia el sol.
                Se orientan y vuelan al norte.

Mi hija despliega sus alas
        Y sigue su norte magnético.

Pásale

"Pásale," she sang from the back seat,
remembering what the Juárez vendor said.
He meant "come in, you'll like what's here."
Galit was only two. We were deep
in the Gila Wilderness, eluding *la migra*,
because we had smuggled Otelia,
a lovely Mexican girl,
to help us with Galit at home.

Later, Otelia was caught at the border.
We never saw her again. My daughter's first loss.
Afterwards, Galit would ride her hobby horse
back and forth, back and forth, in silence.
She would not smile as she rode.

Oh, she was usually a happy child.
I would sing out "pásale" to her,
respond to her smile, the music in her eyes.

Then came the wars of adolescence.
The changes in the restless cells.
Photographs show my daughter shutting down.
Her eyes no longer sang "pásale," or anything else.
Her lilting voice grew loud, strident,
the music harsh and metallic to the ear.

I, who am not a church-going man,
recall my daughter as I walk the banks
of the Río Grande. The river flows south,
carrying the melted winter away.

There is a place inside me where my daughter
dances like these cranes pirouetting in the sun.
Gaining their bearing, they head north.

My daughter lifts up her wings,
rises, and follows her course at last.

"The Motel"

This is a budget motel for truckers
and tourists of the poorer sort.
It has a name but we have always called it
"the motel," as if it were a natural formation,
an outcrop on our lives in Alburquerque.

Although there are no paintings here
of an Indian in a canoe or beside a teepee,
or Chinese workers driving the golden spike
into the railroad spanning the continent,

it is, nevertheless, a good place
for tawdry affairs, for assorted addicts
to hang out and make their deals
beneath landscapes barely a cut or two
above paint by number scenes from nature.

It is close to where my parents live
and convenient also, to hospitals, highways,
shopping centers and close friends.
The comforts here are polyester fringe,
the dangers barely hidden beneath the surface.
This motel, in fact, is very much like America.

⊢•⊕•○•⊕•⊣

Galit came to visit me here once.
A fire broke out in a nearby room.
Firemen in their gas masks
and heavy yellow coats swarmed the motel.
A fire truck with a generator
went up in spectacular flames.
It made the evening news.

All these were *mal agüeros*,
ill omens of doom for us, Galit.
Neither of us knew it
and so it was our small adventure.

Stunned, I sit in this empty room
shrouded by a curtain of unearthly blue.
Outside, a red neon sign blinks
in the fading afternoon. Next door
a man sings in the shower. I hear
an eighteen wheeler on I-40,
Doppler effect of a whine followed by a moan.
A child laughs nearby and then is gone.
I have just come from my daughter.

Crestview Funeral Home

Wrapped in white linen and your prayer shawl,
you travel well, my child,
my silent voyager into the unknown.
The service, traditional, simple,
flows with a dignified drone
for you, my most untraditional daughter.

As the prayers rise and fall,
images come back from a happier time
before this coffin of unvarnished pine,
pegged and with no nails.

Like a burning man in a sea of fire
I grab on to a plank of memory,
recall you and your sisters
traveling with me when I acted
on make-do stages everywhere in New Mexico.

We bounced along two-lane blacktops,
munched down burgers on the run.
Stayed in cheap motels in Raton,
Socorro, Roy, Ruidoso, Taos.
We loved the anarchy of life on the road.

There was that time on the Canadian
I stared down a bull,
mooed to him from the safety of the car.
"Dad, we'd better go," you said
with those large, luminous, olive eyes.

I remember that time in Ruidoso
the conversation-starved man
followed us off the stage.

Stuck his head in the car window
and talked as I quietly slipped into gear,
waved goodbye, then slowly drove away
and he never stopped talking.
We laughed for hours over that.

The thin plank of memory smolders, then burns.
I swim on fire back to the prayers,
the service about to end.
This summing up of my daughter's life.

Oh how I want to grab you and run, Galit.
I want to go on the road with you again,
play all those towns once more.
Drive, drive on forever into the sun.

Fairview Cemetery

Winter clouds sweep in low from the west
this last day of February.
Rain curtains off the volcanic horizon
while to the east, mist and fog shroud the Sandias.

The funeral cortege rolls steadily on.
A drizzle taps a muffled cadence
on the windshields of cars. Lights on,
they wind down to the cemetery gate.

I am a pallbearer unable to think
of my burden in the past tense.
I set my daughter down yet hold on
to the memory of her weight,

the pain in the knuckles of my lifting hand.
I have become the failed acrobat
who has missed the crucial grab for his own daughter.
Now she falls and floats away from me forever.

Her mother, her sisters, and I form
a crumpled family portrait in the rain.
I take handfuls of moist earth
and fling them down on the coffin.

Soon many hands lift and toss
fistfuls of caliche again and again.
Faces pass our impromptu reception line,
offer condolences, then vanish in their cars.

Nearby, a flock of sand hill cranes
rise on silent wings into the dark sky.

North of the Central Avenue Bridge

North of the Central Avenue Bridge,
along the river's edge, trails cut
through thick undergrowth. Grama grass,
cholla, chamisa, goatheads, little blue stem
gather around cottonwoods felled by beaver.

It is late winter, the first days of March.
The river is still cold from snow melt
filtering down the Rio Grande rift
from the Jemez and the Sangre de Cristos.

Where the river flows around a snag of pine,
cottonwood and thistle, a kingfisher perched
on a scraggly branch waits to dive for trout.

Mallards in nervous flight, their sleek bodies
far forward of the thrashing wings, circle once,
swoop down near the undercut left bank.

For hours, the sandhill cranes wheel and turn,
winging north in majestic V's
towards their summer wetlands home.

Somewhere the whine of an electric saw,
the shout of a child and the monotone of traffic
on the Central Avenue Bridge
rise like a symphony to the coming spring.

Just once on a day exactly like this,
I wanted to walk the river bank with you,
to answer your questions about cranes
and about where the river comes from.

Daughter, I am undone by your absence.
All questions and answers dissolve
in a great haloing of wings overhead.
The sandhill cranes circling the sun.

Two Weeks Later, Denton, Texas

While I read at the dining table,
Vered, two years younger
but catching up day by day
to her ageless sister, is in the shower.
This daughter has a deep song,
a true *cante hondo* contagious with life.

What I hear and remember falls like rain.
I think of my daughter María and a son,
another family from another time,
the unpredictable weather in their lives,
and how with love we somehow carry on.

I recall how an apron of water swept down
the Jemez slopes, a melodrama of lightning,
thunderclap and hail in the churning sky.
Afterwards, the calm summer afternoon unfolded.
Vered and her girlfriend came toting
sleeping bags to spend the night in the cabin.

That was years ago. Even then, Galit
kept more to herself in her private space,
a nervous terrain where few birds
lifted wings in sheer joy for flight.
Some cloud blocked the light there.

Now I think of that other shower,
the one that took Galit's and Vered's kin
at Auschwitz and Dachau. Just as darkness
threatens once again to undermine
the thin morning light of day,

a yelp of joy from Mokey, the mixed lab,
signals Vered has emerged from the shower.
She sings to her dog, turns to me, and we talk
of travel plans and road conditions.
I walk to the window, throw open the blinds.

A blue jay drinks a collar of light
from the birdbath in the yard.
Vered and I chatter on about this and that.
and I know I still have a daughter.

Rio Grande

el rio grande
three words in Spanish or English
become the mud red water

the thunderheads with clouds
rain like a wide-skirted
walking woman or
narrow like a thin man

Navajos call this the Mexicans' river and
female river while I prefer the rio bravo
the fearless river south of El Paso

it is the river of potsherds of dreams
a crying woman drowns her children
and looks for them in the mother ditch

her brambled arms grasp the shimmering air
it is the river near the Central Avenue Bridge
where I never find my daughter

blood red water flows over me
watermelon sun of dawn and twilight
rises and sets on the Albuquerque bosque

heat bakes the riverbed
cracks it like weathered shoe leather
the wind sweeps my ashes
across a crow's blank gaze.

Almost Two Years Later

A Boeing 707 like a ghost
flies through the February sky.
It glides through clouds
like the shadow of a fish.
I hear the Doppler fade of its engines.
There's a child on the plane. She glues
her nose to the window before
she disappears in the white curtain above.

Seven hundred and seven days ago,
my daughter left on a day like this.
Small stones rest on her grave nearby.
I look through the falling snow,

try to find her face, to offer her
the only token I have. I lift my arm
and wave goodbye.

.

Four Years Later

(February 25, 1998)

Again, it is a blustery day.
The sun gives no heat, shivers me.
As the morning cold passes
like a ghost through my windbreaker,
I receive a gift from far away.
Sand hill cranes cry in the wind,
circle far above and fly north
as they did four years ago today.
For this gift, I cry.
Daughter, do you hear me?

At Concordia Cemetery, El Paso

(in memory of Galit)

At Concordia Cemetery, El Paso,
near John Wesley Harding's grave
and the Baptist Reverend Reed's,
I think of you. A butterfly

flutters its wings. That small effect
makes an unpredictable wave,
weathers the world and drives a straw
through a tree or sways the sunflower

bending to the pressure of the sun.
You were, you are that impulse.
A zigzag flight to your own beat
across the stars. The Chinese

on the other side of a dividing wall
sleep beneath their solemn stones.
Gunslinger, preacher, the Chinese
tell their tales to the common loam

I hear no song in the border sky.
Silence sings where you have been.
I try to remember your voice
and I hear the chorus of the wind

Tsin Tsun

(recordando a Galit)

Ella volaba por mi vida
como el colibrí,
las alas aleteando veloces
hasta que, al fin,

desilusionada con el mundo,
se fue sin más ni más.
Tsin tsun, palabra
nahuatl para decir

colibrí . . .
el vuelo de mi hija.
Tsin tsun y se fue.

Recuerdo el aire agitado.

Tsin Tsun

(remembering Galit)

She flew through my life
like the hummingbird,
wings at high speed,
until, at last,

disillusioned with the world,
she left suddenly.
Tsin tsun,
Nahuatl word for

hummingbird . . .
the flight of my daughter.
Tsin tsun and she was gone.

I remember the agitated air.

III.

In My
Violin Dream

Y2K

"There's a problem with the Y2K.
Eso es lo que dicen,
that's what they say."

"That's okay. I only drink red."

"¿Cómo que ok? I'm not talking wine."

"Well didn't you say 'white tokay'?"

"Not 'white tokay,' bro. Y2K.
It'll stop your car, panic the feds,
Bring down the power grid."

"That's okay, bro. I'll stick with red."

Matter

(why there is love)

A raindrop beads
on the waxed surface of your car.
It's a universe. A swarm of molecules,
atoms, quarks of all kind,
up quarks, down quarks, charming quarks.

If you get into it, descend
into that world, its heavy traffic,
the busy intersections,
the cramped, humming city
inside the nucleus of an atom,

you'll find wide-open spaces there.
Practically no city at all.
You'll see bits or bytes of things
charming and colorful. They come undone
in a quarky way. Virtual freeloaders,
odd bits of matter ride the quarks
like little cowboys. They can be, or not be,
depending on how you look at them.

Off on the distant particle plains,
there are mountain ranges of almost nothing,
massive in their virtual existence.

You arrive at the smallest bundle of energy
you will ever not see, a shadow of a shadow
of a sort of matter.

If things had been different,
you could have been a contender.

Antimatter

(why there is no love)

That one, the shy one
who looks inside out,
keep an eye on him.
Make sure he doesn't loiter
or sleep under the bridge.
If he gets too close,
you could explode.

Jammin' in a chile house

Parker works over "Cherokee"
stretches out those notes
to unwind that chile house

all the Beats try jammin'
visions into off key
USA of the NRA

America of the death penalty
America of Ak 47's everywhere
America of druggie stuffed jails
America of the shunned insane
America where no one trusts nobody nowhere

no time oh it is a lone note
down this alley
here where wind blows
through down and up
the alto saxophone whims
of your life on wings

like the Bird's flying
between 139th and 140th always
on Seventh Avenue always
and it is December always

the stone-faced wooden Indian
stares at you Europa
you are also an immigrant here

N poem

that's the first letter
      "n"   maybe just a typo
or nth degree of infinity or something

Monk and Coltrane suggested
jammin' back and forth
at the Five Spot Cafe

six months of New York 1957
the Monk played a holy piano
        and the 'trane wasn't a train at all

but an angel on the saxophone
warning even then of apocalypse

surface calm of the fifties
just before the storms broke

tsunamis just off this century's shores

remember that oh you who long
for the Eisenhower years
remember those fake fifties
a typo in history

Monk and Coltrane they knew
they knew

Hilbert's Hotel

We were an enormous horde
Come out of the void to become
Alpha naught, invincible numbers
Stretching forever to infinity.

Our advance guard came to the hotel,
Demanded rooms, tamales, drinks for all.
"My hotel is infinitely full," Hilbert
The owner said. "But I'll tell you what
I can undo. Give me a minute," he said.

He moved guest number one to suite two
And guest number two to suite four.
All the even numbers filled but the odds
Became infinitely empty.

Our horde moved in. Drank all the wine.
Ate all the tamales. We terrorized
The even-numbered guests.
"Don't provoke them," Hilbert said.
"They are as many as you."

We sang the sad corridos,
Offered chicharrón burritos
To our even-numbered bros.
The party didn't last.
Fights broke out.
Even among numbers
Things get irrational.

David Hilbert (1862-1943), a German mathematician, illustrated the concept of infinity with his famous "hotel" which could be infinitely full, yet infinitely empty.

Random Thoughts

I scatter birdseed
on my dad's porch.
Soon a sparrow hops by,
inspects the early Pollock design,
nibbles and flies away.

An unwanted horde of e-mail
infests my computer. I delete
like a crazed serial killer,
or like Huitzilipochtli, warrior god
delighting in my destructiveness.

From a maze of numbers,
a formula, clean as a poem,
organizes chaos into beauty
and balances square roots
on its shoulders, like a Chinese
figurine carrying two baskets
of fish across the Yangstze River.

I want to move
into Hilbert's hotel, every room
full, but an empty one handy,
nearby. I'm tired of being frozen
in amber, my cluttered office
always the same. I'm a figure
on an Anasazi vase
my shadow never moving forever.

Shadow Geometry

Balloon Festival time and
I read Einstein in cold morning light
on the geometry of shadows.

A sphere, a balloon, he says,
casts a shadow on a plane surface.
He's trying to explain space-time curvature
to the math illiterati.

A great balloon, like a gift from Einstein,
floats south in the October sky,
cuts the light streaming from the sun,

casts a flat shadow on the wall.
Einstein smiles from the page,
winks at me, waves goodbye.

On John Conway's "Game of Life"

Imagine a life
without blinkers oscillating on off on off
or gliders inching down the diagonal line
like pixel snails groping towards infinity

Imagine a life
where you die of loneliness
but come back to life if three neighbors
stunned by your absence
bring you back because it's a rule
you can't die like that

Imagine a life
where your daughter never dies
or if she dies she's only turned off
for a while and will be on again before sunset

Imagine a life
where you might reach a steady state
like a traffic light or become a still life
a barge anchored in a calm bay
an abandoned beehive subject only
to the whims of the wind
reflected in a silent pond

Imagine a life
where death is abstract
and only symbols stop breathing
Imagine that

Jack's Bar Revisited

Even the name conveys a lower nobility,
men of the realm, yes, but humble lords
at the tables and booths. Angel the barmaid
serves beer on tap. St. Pauli's Girl
is no match for her. Angel floats
across the bar room floor like the lover's
cruise ship off the Bahamas
in the TV commercial.
She serves the strangers, the good old boys,
the veterans of boozy philosophy.

You drink deeply of that beer,
savor the cold and frothy bite of hops,
malt, barley, the illusion you see
into the world, touch its form.
Your eyes focus on every detail,
the glory and the alcohol of it all.

Angel's curves move you to cry
over your brief mortality, to lament
the loss of the sensual world passing you by.
You want to shout "¡ajuaaa! ¡Y que viva la raza!"
A border crossed you like a wave
long ago, left you stranded like a carnival geek.
You are drunk in a lonely country.

Angel doesn't work here anymore.
The bar has come on evil days.
And the dogs in my neighborhood
are happier than you or me.

Pascualita

At Victoria and Ocampo,
downtown Chihuahua, Mexico,
mannequins in white gowns
stare from the wedding store window
with their blind and stony gaze.

Except for Pascualita. She's the star,
stage center in the wedding store display.
Not a mannequin at all. A real person,
so they say. Embalmed years ago.
A trompe l'oeil masterpiece.

Her hands look human, puffy,
the skin waxy and pale,
as if she were too ill to marry.
She died on her wedding day.

Mother sent her off to Paris,
where, like a creature from a cocoon,
she emerged a white butterfly,
stiff, wings pinned in place,
forever a bride on display.

She stands in her wedding dress,
a fan cools her in the hot Chihuahua sun.
Every strand of natural hair preserved
on her head. She's a superior mannequin,
far above the plaster and fiberglass crowd.

No one notices the assembly line models,
flesh-tinted, with names like "Mari" and
"Modi" (she of the long, fluted neck
minus her head). These old Greneker

plaster casts, the hand-me-down
Hindsgaul girls, long to be elegant
things, lovely brides of flesh and bone.

Jealous in their fright wigs,
they see the crowds at night,
the novios who pray to Pascualita.
"We who never lived," the mannequins say,
"dream the dreams of Pascualita.
Our poorly made hands, cast hurriedly
in common clay, reach out to you.
When you walk away, give us
at least a backward glance."

Golden Viscacha Rat

I miss the salt plains.
The streets of the city are harsh,
here where I escaped the trap.
Near the trash bin
I find spilled popcorn,

eat it for the salt.
There's water in the gutter.
I have no need for it.
I need only succulent plants,
shade where I can sleep.

Did these two-legged giants
trap me for my golden hair?
They fill the streets,
buildings, cars.
They kill everywhere,
every plant, every animal,
including themselves,
but they love blondes.

I miss the salt plains,
the cool nights and fiery days,
my peaceful life as a golden rat.

Mouse on campus

you try hard
to write a poem

look at that mouse darting
across the university mall

healthy little guy
miguelito ratón

on a romp
all big ears and furry coat

he doesn't write history
or reflect on ancestral shadows

he is Immanuel Kant's mouse
a form that hunts forever after itself

the mousiness of it all
corn smell yellow teeth

rosary bead eyes
whiskers feet and tail

the cat will regurgitate
Calabi Yau space mouse

amphibole mouse who pops
into and out of existence

like you and me

Sugar in the Raw

Sugar packet says
"Sugar in the Raw,
Natural Cane from Hawaii."
Impatient poem,
won't wait for paper,

says, "I'm turbulent
like turbinado sugar.
I'm raw, rough and sweet,
in a small packet.

"Like honey,
I don't need refrigeration.
I'm good anytime.

"Write me down now,
on the palm of your hand
or on this sugar packet.
I'll keep forever."

In my hippie party dream

(or my selfish bastard dream)

My wife leaves town for the weekend.
"Drive my car," she says, "if you want to."
She goes and the hippies appear.
Six to eight of them. They smile and laugh.
We have a party. It goes on for days.
"You have two cars. Can we borrow one?"
"Sure," I tell the hippie girl.
"Take my wife's, the white one." She does.

The hippies come back. I see the car.
"Oh shit," I think. They have painted
my wife's car with bright hippie colors,
green and purple flowers, rainbows,
hippie peace signs everywhere. My wife
will be back soon. I know.

"Why did you do that?" I ask.
The hippies smile and disappear.
The car is there in its bright new colors.
My wife will be back soon.

In my northern flight dream

My wings strain against the gray slate
skies. Wisps of clouds stream out
behind me. An iceberg tip
rises in the Beaufort Sea.

Off to starboard wing, another bird
spurs me on with his cry.
My raptor eyes take in the dying sun.
I don't know why, but I must take back
one piece of ice to a warmer land.
I spot an iceberg below, fold my wings,
dive, and ignore unforgiving hard edges.

The last ice crystal melts on my tongue
as I wake up in my bed. A dream,
but I still savor the cold taste, the ice
that almost made it into this world.

Light-headed poem

This afternoon on my walk,
shoelace undone, I raised my foot
to a bench, leaned to tie the shoe,
and listed like the Titanic
going down. A woman looked to see
if I was drunk. It could be
the world is lighter, a balloon
untethered to drift in clouds,
a ship with a broken rudder.
It sails everywhere, nowhere.

My dizziness is oppressive.
My light-headed room sways
to swing music from the forties.
Tonight, I'll try not to spin
in my sleep. Stand on deck.
Keep a sharp lookout
for a pitfall in the dark:
the weak-walled vein
about to give way to the red
flood, paralysis, the slide
into idiocy. Or infinity.
Or nothing at all.

Fed Ex Blues

Inscrutable Fed Ex message:

"Call the 1-800 number and say
the five digit routing code." I call.

Computer voice: "Say the number slowly."
I say: 0 0 0 5 0.

Computer voice: "You said: 37186."
No, no I say. I said no such thing.

Computer voice: "Please repeat the numbers."
This time, I mince no numbers. 0 0 0 5 0

Computer voice: "I don't understand you.
Please use the number pad on your phone."

I use the number pad: 00050
Computer voice: "You didn't press the pound sign."

I press 00050, then the pound sign.
Computer voice: "You must say this number.

Speak slowly to confirm."
I say: 0 0 0 5 0.

Computer voice: "You said: 49263."
No, no I say. I said no such thing.

Computer voice: "Please repeat the numbers."
I say: Snirgle. Blat. Biffo. Blot. Zinkle Guf.

Computer voice: "You said: 00050.
The item has been shipped.

You should receive it.
If you have questions, please use

our voice automated system.
Practice your enunciation.
Thank you."

In My Violin Dream

The concert violinist can't play.
His fingers are numb. He's my friend.

I tell him I will take his place and
play the Bach Solo for Violin.
Everything will be okay.

He mumbles "thank you" and says
"I'm off to the cocktail party.
Everything will be okay."

I will play the Bach Solo for Violin.
It bothers me, I don't know
how to hold the violin.

It's difficult for a left-handed person.
I've got time to get the hang of it.
Everything will be okay.

Meanwhile, horses run
through the auditorium.
"We've got big bucks on this,
We expect you to fill this place."

"Not to worry," I tell the promoter.
"I will play the Bach Solo for Violin.
I will play it well."

It bothers me, I don't know
the Bach Solo for Violin.
I must learn to read music.

The horses gallop out of the auditorium.
Everyone's back from the cocktail party.

I'd better learn to play,
I think to myself.
The audience is restless.

Backstage I hear murmurs,
the critical coughs.   The curtain opens.
Wild applause for the violin virtuoso.
I raise the bow, put string to string,
and scratch an off-key sound.

I drench the Bach Solo for Violin
in the aloof sweat of dreams.

"I could sure use some karaoke," I say.
The audience laughs. "I tried to play this
once in a row boat," I say.

More laughter from the audience.
Maybe they'll think I'm a comedian.

IV.

With the Eyes
of a Raptor

Anabasis or the March Up Country

> *. . . at this moment, the barbarians came upon them*
> *and down from the hilltop discharged their missiles*
> *and sling-stones and arrows, fighting under the lash.*
>
> — Xenophon, Anabasis
> Fourth century, B.C.

Sun. Pain. Dust. Sweat. Slog on.
I am poor, from a small town in Thrace.
I enlisted in the army. All day
We march. Swollen feet. Thirst.
I dislike this camp. The dirt. The heat.
My first day here is like my birth.
I came screaming and bloody to this place.
Alone. I know no one. Where I was
Before I was born, I don't know.
My mind's a blank map before this camp.

I have no idea where my orders
Come from or who writes them.
Every day someone here is killed
By a sword thrust or an arrow
From some ambush in the hills. The populace
Hates us. They smile as we bury our dead.
Tomorrow we march in line of battle across
Those mountains above, the rivers, streams,
The dry plain to the Aegean Sea.
Soon we break camp. Post the guard.

I will not see Thrace again.

On the Eve of War

A boy with a dyed red
mohawk drinks his coffee,
flirts with girls smelling of rain.

He has studied his gestures
in the mirror, like the President.
The Albuquerque sky,

mistress to the sun, is dark today,
cold drizzle running off her shoulders.
We enjoy the young people
noisy, laughing in the coffee shop.

Why do I drift off to Warsaw,
1939? Jack-booted troops
knock down my door in a dream.
My country has gone away.

Vuelo a Guadalajara

30 de noviembre, 1994

Instalados en el avión,
vuelo de Dallas a Guadalajara,
se sienta a mi lado
una abuela mexicana.
Tiene hijos en Texas
mas su corazón está
en San Juan de los Lagos.

Al levantar vuelo el avión,
la abuela se pone a rezar.
Murmurando su rosario
me mira un poco de reojo:
¿Y tú no rezas?"

"Sí" . . . le digo, y en seguida añado
para cambiar de tema:
"Mira que maravillosas nubes."

"Ave María," responde la señora.
El avión se sacude
como si sufriera un escalofrío.
"reza por nosotros . . ."
sigue el runrún del rosario.

Entonces llegan los golpes inesperados.
Fantasmas de cuervos se ven graznando
por las ventanillas del avión tembloroso.

"Ahora y en la hora de nuestra muerte . . ."
Somos dos sombras veloces
atravesando el cielo mexicano.

Ella sigue con su rosario
y yo con mis silencios cargados de historia.
¿Cómo decirle a esta abuela
que ya no creo en las grandes narrativas?

El vuelo se suaviza.
Aterrizamos en Guadalajara.
La tierra firme sube como vino viejo
por nuestras piernas agradecidas.

Se despide la señora
como si fuera mi propia abuela.
"Que le vaya bien, señor,
y no seas malcria'o."

Flight to Guadalajara

(November 30, 1994)

Aboard the flight
from Dallas to Guadalajara,
a Mexican grandmother
sits down beside me.
She has sons in Texas
but her heart is in San Juan de los Lagos.

The moment the plane lifts off,
she begins to pray.
Murmuring her beads,
she looks at me suspiciously:
"Don't you pray?"

"Yes" . . . I say to her.
"Look at those marvelous clouds,"
trying to change the subject.

"Hail Mary," the grandmother says.
The airplane shakes
as if a chill ran down its spine.
"Pray for us . . ."
she murmurs away at her rosary.

Then come the unexpected blows.
Ghosts of crows caw along the windows
of the trembling airplane.

"Now and in the hour of our death . . ."
We are two swift shadows
cutting across the Mexican sky.

She continues with her rosary
and I with my silence laden with history.
How can I say to this grandmother
I no longer believe in the grand narratives?

The flight becomes smooth again.
We land in Guadalajara.
The solid earth rises like an old wine
through our grateful legs.

She takes leave of me
as if she were my own grandmother.
"May it go well with you, sir,
and don't be a bad boy."

El Fantasma del Hotel Mendoza

Guadalajara, México
1 de diciembre, 1994

El fantasma del Hotel Mendoza
toca esta noche.
Las teclas del piano se mueven
como si por su propia cuenta.

Es piano moderno accionado
por discos de computadora.
El fantasma toca como viejo
piano de cilindro,
toca jazz, toca los blues.

De niño tocaba en fiestas familiares.
Después se agitaron las teclas
en México, París, y Londres.

En su día fue amigo de Fats Waller,
de Art Tatum (el Tatum),
de Bessie Smith y del famoso
"Duque" Ellington.
Charlie Bird hablaba bien de él.

Ahora los huéspedes
ignoran el fantasma.
El sigue tocando
ritmos de los blues
desde un rincón del ciberespacio.

El fantasma del Hotel Mendoza
toca musica
herida por el pasado.

Sus manos caen
como dos pájaros del tiempo
muertos sobre las teclas.
Se quedan algunas notas
aleteando en la nada.

The phantom in the Hotel Mendoza

Guadalajara, Mexico
December 1, 1994

The phantom of the Hotel Mendoza
is playing tonight.
The piano keys move
as if of their own accord.

It's a modern piano
controlled by computer discs.
The phantom plays it
like an old player piano.
He plays jazz, he plays blues.

As a child he played the local fiestas.
Later the piano keys flew
in Mexico City, Paris, London.

He was Fats Waller's friend,
Art Tatum, too, in his day.
Friend of Bessie Smith
and Duke Ellington.
Charlie "Bird" Parker spoke well of him.

Now the guests
ignore the phantom.
He just keeps playing
the blues from some corner
of cyberspace.

The phantom of the Hotel Mendoza
plays music
wounded by the past.

His hands fall
like two birds of time,
dead upon the keyboard.
A few notes
still flutter in the void.

Old Woman at the Genealogy Center

She parks her grey vintage Dodge on the third try.
A rag doll, she emerges in slow motion
from her car. Propped up on her aluminum cane,
she trembles, a leaf about to fall,
and inches her way to the Genealogy Center.

After all, she is a child. Her playmates,
family, call from bygone centuries.
If she could only shrug off her coat,
her second-hand rose dress,
trade in the white hair for blond,
renew the flaccid dugs, the nipples
circumspect from lack of desire,
feel her skin taut and glowing once more.

One good twist of the hips, a missed step,
And she's free. People rush to help her
But she doesn't need them. She tosses her cane
At a gaping man. Does a hand spring.
She's dancing now, like Ginger with Fred
In a forties flick. The light goes green

And I turn from the Genealogy Center.
She's free. I'll never see her again.

Liberación

For Perry and Carolyn

Shaula is radiant to starboard,
Scorpio poised to bite.

This afternoon blue gills
Nibble on my belly.
I swim lazy circles around
Liberación at anchor in
Elephant Butte Lake.

I reflect
On the fifty-seven stars
Sailors use to locate themselves
On the surface of the sea.

Early in the day we are in irons,
The sails flap and fall silent.
Hard tiller to port
Catches the wind.
We sail again.

I'm not sure what "liberación" means.
It has something to do with the way
The sea holds the boat fast
And lets it go the next moment.

It has something to do with blue gills,
The way they nibble at me
As I swim circles that drift
Into question marks in my wake.

It has something to do
With staying out of irons.
Push the tiller hard.
Cut into the wind.

Liberación
Tonight I break bread
With Shaula and the stars.

The elephant island
Circled by this artificial lake
Stands in great silence.
Trapped in stone, the elephant
Moves with geologic dignity.
His bulk mirrored in water
Fragments into light,
Dances off the waves
Toward the hills beyond.

I speak to him.
He understands.

In the San Antonio Hotel

In the San Antonio Hotel,
Juárez, Mexico, Sunday night,
I drink my tequila straight.

The bartender talks and I listen
con respeto. He has survived
Mexico and its transformations.

Díaz and the Positivists gave way
to Villa y la revolución.
He remembers wagon trains

moving north from Chihuahua to Juárez,
the breadlines in Torreón.
Durante la revolución,

he stood all night to buy bread
at five in the morning.
By six all the bread was gone.

¿Y la revolución? Well, it gave way to PRI,
he says. That is why we are here tonight
at the bar of the San Antonio Hotel.

The bartender talks his way
back through the decades to his youth.
My mind's first photograph

records the black hair, the sharp cheekbones,
black fire opal eyes. The snapshots
show softer features, grey and pudgy,

many folds and wrinkles.
He has become something like resignation,
his eyes gone to grandfatherly gentle.

There are only three of us in the bar.
The bartender, another mexicano, and myself.
Later, back in my third floor room,

I throw open the window.
The green and red fluorescent sign
of the Intermezzo Bar

jabs me like a thumb in the eye.
My only companion for the night
is a bottle of wine I brought from El Paso.

You must drink it, the bartender said.
because you can't take it back
across the border. The thick moon

coats the sky with a pale glaze,
the blurred narrative between dark and dawn.
I peer across the river to the USA.

The Rio Grande purls alone
through El Paso, the space between
two worlds. A door slams. A moving car

fades away. In the distance I hear a train
lament in a long moan on the border.

Canyon, Texas Sestina

Cope's Coney Island Café has a steak
Well worth waiting for. You walk
West along fourth avenue and two
Blocks later you come across the plain
Café. You enter, sit, and watch the road,
Here where steaks and earth are red as clay.

You recall, nearby, that other red clay,
The Palo Duro where boys in blue drove a stake
Through the Comanche's heart. End of the road
For dead horses and the tribe. Then the walk
Into captivity. Crossing the plain,
They staggered on, one at a time, or two.

Now the ghosts of tribes and Mexicans, too,
Bake in the Texas sun. Souls of clay
Rise from the earth, fall back to the plain.
The deep Palo Duro Canyon is a mistake,
It seems, on the flat surface where you walk
On a line scratched in the dirt. Call it a road.

Many's the time you will think of this road
And wonder what burial ground it leads to.
Children of bygone ghosts now walk
Over ancestors graves deep in the clay.
You reflect on this and chew your tender steak
Here in the Coney Island Café. It's plain

You need hours and days to explain
How memory suddenly floods the road.
Cope's Coney Island Café grilled steak
Tastes better than history. Harsh, too,
is Texas, like a hail stone pounding the clay,
Like the starved Comanches on their dreadful walk.

Ah, but that was then. Few people walk
Anywhere these days. They ride across the plain
On paved highways that sanitize the clay.
No one cares about the bad old road
When the new one whisks you away to
A feast of drink and hearty steak.

Recall, you are clay walking the long walk.
A ghost will spoil your steak on the plain.
And you will join the dust of buffalos, too.

El Exiliado

Se va soñando de plátanos
en país cubierto de nieve.

Arrastra el madero de la memoria
por las calles desconocidas del exilio.

Se marea en el desierto
donde navega por alto mar.

Comienza a perder su idioma
en hilos de voces que se deshacen.

Cuando oye la bocina del barco,
es él quien se pierde en la nieblina.

The Exile

He dreams of bananas
in a snow-covered land.

He drags the cross of memory
through unknown streets of exile.

He becomes seasick in the desert
where he navigates through high seas.

He begins to lose his language
in threads of voices unraveling.

When he hears the ship's whistle,
it is he who is lost in the fog.

El Exiliado, II

Si es norteño desterrado al sur,
sueña de color blanco, de nieve,
al contemplar el vuelo del guacamayo.

Es niño que mama al pecho
de loba desconocida.
Jamás oye los aullidos de su manada.

El exiliado, cuando habla o escribe
con sus compatriotas,
es mensaje urgente de radio clandestino.

Si se muere en el desterrado,
se vuelve astronauta dando vueltas
por espacios negros y dolorosos.

The Exile, II

If he's a northerner exiled to the south,
he dreams of the color white, of snow,
when he contemplates a flight of macaws.

He is a child nursing at the teats
of a she-wolf he does not know.
He never hears the cry of his wolf pack.

When the exile speaks
or writes to his compatriots,
he is the urgent message
from a clandestine radio.

If he dies in exile,
he becomes an astronaut
circling through dark and painful spaces.

Sueño del Exiliado

El guitarrista toca un corrido
en caja de madera sin cuerdas.
Allá desde el horizonte
se acerca un buque de vela.

Es buque de alto mar,
alto cielo a toda vela.
Vuela el buque sin moverse,
sin salir del sueño.

El buque es viejo,
del siglo dieciseis.
Se deshace en nubes
que se quiebran en pedazos
de rompecabezas abandonadas,
desaparecidas en la nada.

Siguen llegando buques
uno tras otro. El guitarrista
toca el corrido que no se oye.

También canta el guitarrista.
Canta en silencio.

The Exile's Dream

The guitarist strums a ballad
on a wooden box with no strings.
From the far horizon
a sailing ship comes on.

Ship of the high seas,
sky under full sail.
Ship that flies without moving,
never leaving the dream.

Sailing ship, relic
of the sixteenth century,
it comes undone in clouds
breaking up into pieces
of abandoned puzzles
lost in the void.

Ships continue to arrive,
one after the other. The guitarist
plays the ballad no one hears.

The guitarist also sings.
He sings in silence.

Guadalupe Hidalgo

how beautiful these vowels sing
the ahs oohs and ohs please the ear

the way a line drawn in the sand
loves your eye or better still

the spiral shape the concertina wire
strung along the border takes

the treaty is paper thin
fits you like a Mexican wrestler's mask

it hides the botched surgery of politics
the hard edged scar of the border

you are kin to Dr. Frankenstein's monster
badly stitched together by the State

threads of English and Spanish dangle
from your lips and you are sliced

north and south right down the middle
you look for bits of your family's flesh

along the curbstones of barrio streets
from deep behind your epicanthic folds

you walk the broken landscape of memory
your indio eyes scan the daguerreotype

de tu familia who wave in sepia tone
from both sides of the border

they disappear into time and chance
you call to each other through a fog

si muero lejos de tí you recall Kearny's
boys in faded blue "not a pepper

not an onion shall we take" he lied
si muero lejos de tí remember the good priest

Martínez from Taos cut off from Mexico and Spain
the spine of his culture broken in half

guadalupe hidalgo mere words
in a long line of lies

you know the wind buries the line in the sand
the concertina wire rusts back to earth

I swear the broken spine is mending itself
it's growing back together

it's growing back together.

Proposición 187

(Como dicen en las películas,
si hay una semblanza entre este poema
y una petición política,
es por pura casualidad.)

Desde el principio tuvimos suerte.
Echamos afuera a los mexicanos indocumentados.
Después expulsamos a los mexicanos americanos,
indios, hispanos, latinos de toda estirpe.

En seguida acabamos con los negros,
los judíos, los católicos,
y hasta con los protestantes.

Entonces a los japoneses, chinos,
y todo asiático, se les llegó su hora.
Inútil que algún sueco, noruego

o hindú tratara de esconderse
entre nosotros de mirada serena.
Todos acabaron en el extranjero.

Para no alargar el cuento,
Al fin quedamos tú y yo.

Tú de ojos azules
pero manchados de color ambiguo.

Tú de pelo rubio
aunque con unas trenzas
morenas y sospechosas.

Sé que me tienes miedo,
que vigilas mis armas
contando cada bala.

Mas cálmate ya, mujer.
Sin tí no hubiera nadie
con quien lucir
mi limpieza de sangre.

Habrá tiempo para morirnos.
Se quedará este país
como modelo de un mundo amplio,
sin gente, desolado, perfecto.

Proposition 187

(Like they say in the movies,
any resemblance between this poem
and real politics
is purely coincidental.)

We were lucky from the beginning.
We kicked out the undocumented Mexicans.
We expelled the Mexican Americans,
Indians, Hispanics, Latinos of all types.

We finished off the African Americans,
the Jews, the Catholics,
and even the Protestants.

Then it was their turn –
the Japanese, the Chinese,
every Asian. In vain
did some Norwegian or Swede,

or Hindu try to hide
among us whose gaze is serene.
They were sent to foreign lands.

To make a long story short,
only you and I are left.

You with your blue eyes
stained with some ambiguous color.

You with your blond hair
although some of the strands
are dark and suspicious.

I know that you fear me.
You keep watch over my weapons.
You count every bullet.

Be calm, woman.
I need you.
So I can display
my purity of blood
to someone.

We'll have plenty of time to die.
This country will serve as a model
for a bountiful world.
Without people, desolate, perfect.

I drive my pickup truck

I drive my pickup truck
and wonder about epistemology
on this balmy January day.
I've read this essay by A. J. Ayer,
dry old logical positivist,
but very witty at times. Not dry at all.
I don't believe him. The thing is

it's Saturday in Albuquerque. I daydream,
drive on automatic pilot.
I always travel out of body
but when I drive my pickup truck
on a balmy day supposed to be cold,

I don't care if I don't have
a theory of knowledge. Or of being.
It's hard rock on the singing wire
on KUNM. I get into the
hey ya, hey ya, hey ya ho.

I feel sorry for all the Indians
I killed when I was a kid.
And guilty for cheering the cowboys
who always beat the Mexicans
and Indians in the movies.

Left turn onto Central. Shift,
cruise past Garcia's Restaurant.
The little toy Mexican
with his bottle of beer
dances round and round
where he hangs on
my rear view mirror.

To hell with ontology.
It's a great winter day.

Wild Birds

(for Patricia Clark Smith)

Once you showed me a poem
with geese flying north at winter's end.
Another time, you pointed out the sandhill cranes
who lifted up on their wings
a sorrow I carried alone. You taught
me the seasons of wild birds.

Now I stand in my daughter and son-in-law's
backyard. They are proud of the wedding gift
you gave them. A pond for small fish.
A good place to be at the end of a Boise summer day.

The sun shrinks to a red-breasted finch on the horizon.
Out of that sky a mallard duck and his mate
dive down to nest in the pond.

Daughter, husband, and father
beam like children. I catch my breath and recall
this is your kind of moment. And I know
it is good to be here in the world.

The grackles of San Antonio

The grackles of San Antonio
sing the River Walk into dusk.
Their varied cries
recall a pastoral time

long before this city scene,
the smog-filled urban sky.
Most unloved of birds,
the loud, blank shot

startles you into flight.
You befoul the streets, the passers-by,
as you fly like a black cloud
across the face of the lowering sun.

You settle down in the dark trees
like dreams waiting for the night.

For Ricardo

(Ricardo Moya 1938-2003)

Ricardo, you understand how I return
to my old love, the word, the lines of this world.
My son is safe in this realm. Wives, lovers,
children, live forever their tragicomic
dramas in this white expanse of paper
dusted by blobs of ink, wind-blown codes.
Este corrido de la familia fills the empty space
with music, songs. Your guitar is a voice
torn from the pages of suffering.

Ricardo, there's a wound in the Taos night
of your guitar. You sing the barely remembered
cantinas of lost love, the metaphors
of tender women, la política,
the unfinished revolution. Otra cerveza
por favor. La del estribo.

Ricardo, this is the country of no memory.
You take your last stand against silence,
the bourgeois politeness about despair.
You praise los batos locos, Mexican dreams
of love and death and freedom.

Ricardo, no wonder Plato barred
poets from his Republic. You have the right
to consume, to not be yourself in America.
You know this. Your guitar subverts
the "one culture" pendejada. Six doves
fly out from your strumming fingers.
Adiós, Ricardo, y que seas malcria'o.

Boise to Denver in the rain, in the dark

I am highway beat
all the way from Boise
driving in the dark,

rain and lightning
slapping me hard in the face.
Ahead is the glow of Cheyenne,

a promise of sleep
off Interstate 70,
where I do not want to die.

But it's Frontier Days again.
The yearly cowboy fiesta
brings the crowds to town.

Cars and covered wagons
fill the parking lots beneath
NO VACANCY signs.

I see soggy red Cheyenne
through my rearview mirror,
tune in KUVO, keep time

to the old great jazz,
stay alive in the right lane,
stay awake to the windshield wipers.

That night I miss the Denver flood
by one Bird and a long Coltrane.
No rest from Boise to Denver.

Winter poem

Winter begins with a finch
pecking at the suet my wife
puts on the desert willow for small birds.

Clouds feathered black and white
like the finch and his kin
whirl in the December sky.

No cat lies in wait for the finch.
No Cooper's hawk is poised
talons ready for the kill.

There is no violence.
Only the cold like a fat lover
rolls over, enfolds us in her silence.

Poem for Christmas

In another season of war,
I hear the distant missiles, the planes
Launch from aircraft carriers. The news
Is bad. Always. Everywhere.
I turn off the TV, step outside.
Gray clouds color the trees in a silver patina.
My neighbor's geese honk in distress.

A low whistle, a curious song, relieves
The drabness of it all. There beneath
The desert willow branch, a nuthatch
In his black crown and white face mask,
Walks up the tree. He pays no heed
To the rise and fall of the stock market,
The fate of corporate thieves, the injunctions
To buy, to consume. The nuthatch
Walking up the trunk of the desert willow:
A visual gift for the season of giving.

Mary Cassatt

She paints the reflection
of a redhead looking at herself
in a gilded mirror. I see the reflection
of the painting of the woman
looking at herself in the gilded mirror

on a tv screen. My reflection there,
my image, grey-haired and glassy,
a vague version of myself, observes
as I watch the reflection of the image, pixels
spat out by the electron gun, of Mary Cassatt's
painting of the woman looking at herself
in the mirror. It stares darkly at me,
this image of myself, my disembodied self.

In these words, dear reader, do you see
only letters, a soon-to-be-forgotten alphabet
scrawled by a shadow of a shadow?
Or do the words pull out of the magic hat
inside your head, a mysterious rabbit,
yourself in the gilded mirror, newborn, raw?
Do the words reach out, grab you by the hand,
lead you into this painting, this one?

Near Ocean City, New Jersey

I walk along the beach
waves drum up a chorus in the sand
a song for the sea gull
his swooping dive
the age-old smell of sex
hangs over the wet centuries
of high and low tides

some glimmering thing
dances in the corner of my eye
a fish like a thin spray of silver
leaps in the white foam
a wave scoops it up
slams it down on the beach
to shudder at my feet

the sea gull lands in seconds
his knowing eye fixes
on this late morning meal
the fish gasps at the world
gone suddenly dry
we stare at each other numbed
by all that separates us

the sea gull will not wait
I take a deep breath
grab the fish as best I can
fling him back into the Atlantic

death's bird shimmering with light
like fresh linen on the clothesline
flutters his wings and flies
a lazy circle over the beach

he will carry off
some small fish today
in a blaze of whiteness

I walk on towards Ocean City
alert to my ancient kinsmen
beneath the surface of the sea
angels overhead invisible
against the sun
close their wings
to dive and fall upon our hearts
to do what they must

L. B. J.'s (little brown jobs)

Finches and sparrows gather at the feeder
While above the sun wings to the west.
Here is the place in the nice poem
For children to run through the sprinklers
And toss the Frisbee to the dog. Call him

Sparkie. But the dog died years ago
And besides, this isn't summer.
The children have long since grown.
You can see their pictures
In almost every room. So what is left?

Why the finches and sparrows of course.
Now a Cooper's hawk appears from nowhere.
He sits on our front yard fence, eyes focused
On the feeder, his long yellow talons

Poised to spring on any unwary bird. Are you
Ready for the grim sequel to this scene?
The sudden attack, the flurry of feathers,
The screams. Blood on the snow.
Ah well, you know the rest.

You like that, don't you? Another war movie
In your head. The boys with fixed bayonets.
Lots of flags. Glory hallelujah
Etc., etc., and etc.

Always some joker in a suit
Or dressed like a soldier screaming:
"Today a finch.
Tomorrow the world!"

Scrub Jay

I set peanuts out for him and his small tribe.
He flies from telephone pole to wire to twig
to porch railing. He is fearless, if it is a he,
head well-formed, with Apache tear eyes.
He carries his own banner of grey underbelly,
blue wings. Somewhere in the yard

He buries the peanuts. Tries to remember
where they are for the winter ahead.
We have stared eye to eye for a long time,
or so it seems. His song is a harsh rasp.
I sing mine in words he has no need to hear.
Suddenly he's a dart through the air,

disappears in the elm. I am left alone
with the compressed movie of my life. I fast
forward beginning to end, surround the flash
of blue with my immense ignorance of the jay.

Recordando a Rebecca García y Gutiérrez de Devine

"Todo el día en el camino. It took all day
to go by carreta from Old Town to Carnuel."

So says my grandmother as she sits
in her rocking chair on the porch.
She watches the eighteen wheelers
truck by on New York Avenue.

"Tengo muchos parientes en Carnuel
y allá por Chililí," she says.

My grandmother gazes off to
the last century. Her eyes are
weathered like wagon wheels,
brown like deep rutted trails,
as patient as the earth itself.

"What did you learn today, mi 'jito?
'Oh, nothing, grandma."

"We would visit con Juan y Luisa.
Los García y los Gutiérrez
tenían muchos terrenos."

She rocks faster. Rolls
a Rizla straw paper and lights up.
"Mira, mi 'jito, you be a good boy."

"Yo tenía parientes que los apaches
llevaron cautivos." She wraps herself
in her shawl. From inside a cloud of smoke
she thinks east, searches the plains
for her captive relatives,

for the cautivos, the lost children,
the lost land. "Grandma,
were you alive during the Civil War?"

"No mi 'jito." She laughs.
The burnt ash of history falls
from her cigarette. I think she's afraid

I'll forget to tell her stories of Carnuel,
forget to be a good boy,

forget Tijeras Canyon, the cautivos,
the road from Old Town to the mountains.

Grandma, I try to remember your stories.
The way you rolled your Zig-Zag tobacco
into frail cigarettes. The way the long ash
hangs now only from my memory.
Grandma, I am not a good boy.
Please forgive me.
I try not to forget.

With the Eyes of a Raptor

I.

I read the letter
with the eyes of a raptor.

My great-grandfather,
don Epimenio, writes
to his daughter Alicia,
my grandmother:

II.

Observatory Ranch
Wagon Mound, New Mexico
May 24, 1925

"Dear Alicia,

I hope that you and Ed
and the boys are well.
Everyone here is in good health.
I would like you to buy flowers
there, in Raton. My cousin Rafael
will bring them to Wagon Mound
to place on Porfiria's grave
on Memorial Day.

And please send flowers
for my mother's grave in Taos.

I thought about coming to Wagon Mound
for Memorial Day
but I am behind with the planting
and the fences, so
I will not be there on the twenty-eighth.

May all be well with you.
With love, your father,

Epimenio Martínez."

III.

Alicia reads your letter,
don Epimenio. She folds it,
puts it in a drawer
where it sleeps for years
wrapped in a blanket of dust.
She is the young mother
who longs to visit with you,
who feeds, clothes, and schools
her five children and comforts
her coal miner husband.

Dutiful daughter,
she buys flowers for Porfiria,
also for Epimenio's mother.
She hides her disappointment
you must tend to the planting and fences
and will not be there on the twenty-eighth.
A child screams.
My father? An uncle?

Her children branch out
from her fingertips into the cities.
The future smells of oil and steel,
railroads and sweatshops.
Ghosts of oak and poplar trees
blossom only in her dreams.

Observatory Ranch spirals
into her private mythology.
She remembers trips to Europe,
the Spanish hacienda,
her private schools in St. Louis.
The dried-out hide of the past
becomes fine leather in her mind.

Alicia tends to her family
while you, don Epimenio,
plant crops and mend fences.
History turns yellow and brittle
in this letter I hold
like a bird of prey.

IV.

Seventy years later
Ed and the boys
along with Alicia
are at ease. They are dead,
as is cousin Rafael.

Forgive me, don Epimenio.
I intrude on your privacy
with talons and a fierce eye.
I am the predator historian

who takes your words in flight,
tears them away from the past.
I need those words now.

Don Epimenio, if I could,
I would shake you and the dead
out of this brittle page
to swirl like dry leaves
or young birds with strong wings.

I bring your letter from the hunt
back to my nest of documents.
I feed the contents back to you,
the words regurgitated,
to fill the beaks of the dead,
the remembered family.
I want you to fly again.

V.

Somewhere I am writing:

Don Epimenio,

You need not worry
about the planting and the fences.
Wheat chaff swirls in the fields.
The fallen posts shelter
ants, mice, and the devil's claw.
They turn to earth again.

There is no need to tell
Alicia and Ed and the boys
to be anywhere by the twenty-eighth.

They are here in the torn bits
of voices, the scraps of song
whirled about inside my head.

This century dies, don Epimenio.
You need not worry about flowers.
Vendors sell basketfuls of
daisies, carnations, roses, gladiolas
at the entrances to cemeteries.

And the wildflowers, the asters,
lobelia, primroses, columbines,
grow everywhere. So many
of our kin have died, the earth itself
has become a vast camposanto.

Don Epimenio, I truly know
the hunger in your words.
A missing daughter
shadows my future.

I hope these lines
will sustain us for a while
in this nest of memory.
It is not too much to ask
before my eyes glaze over.

Before I close my wings
and dive, dive.

Diesel Fuel Moon

Diesel fuel moon
over Albuquerque.
I inhale the silver fumes.
Open space all gone.
Esos cuentos de mi abuela
all gone, all gone.
But let me tell you . . .

V.

The Discourse of
Little Dog
and
Big Dog

I. Little Dog Barks

Little Dog howls aauuu!
He wails for his own kind,
his kin without history
who recall the great pack
running in the snow.
His bark is a sharp jab. It nags
like a failed revolution.
This time no firing squad shoots
no rebel up against the wall.
He barks for his daily walk.

Time for Big Dog to walk Little Dog.
Big Dog runs with the sheep.
He laps up what tidbits he finds
in the metal pan of his memory.
He tries to seek out his doggy dreams
where forepaws have never gone before.
Little Dog perks up his ears,
alert for the coming walk.
Big Dog pockets a bone for Little Dog,
reserves memory to gnaw on for himself.

Little Dog is a black mix of a mutt.
Part lab. Part chow. Twentieth century
American roadside dog who appeared
out of an Oklahoma rainstorm.
He growls at lowering clouds. Fears tornados.
Little Dog, always irritated, always irritating,
barks because he wants to go for his walk.

Time for the two dogs to walk.
The fat, graying one, Big Dog,
old coyote, not the Santa Fe kind

found in curio shops for tourists,
but the real thing, genuine Chicano coyote
loping at the edge of his vanishing world.
And Little Dog, Midwest mongrel
who believes in the world of smell,
the sanctity of touch.

Big Dog has a canine security number,
a doghouse, various mates over time,
a cell phone, a computer, a modest SUV.
He works in a large, scenic kennel
at the suburban edge of the urban sprawl.

Big Dog is as American as hot dog,
"perro caliente," the Spanish dictionary says,
"abominable food of the North Americans."
He scratches himself, like any other dog,
thinks mostly . . . about himself.
Secretly hates his modest SUV.
Loves his wife's gourmet cooking.
"Great frozen pizza," Big Dog
says to his wife. "Frozen yourself,"
wife says. She hopes they'll go for a walk.

II. The Red Leash

"Go for a walk, Little Dog?
Let's go for a walk!
¡Vámonos, perrito!"
Big Dog hears the throaty bark,
sees the nervous twirling tail.
Little Dog slobbers and says with his eyes
"Yes, Big Dog, yes, yes!

Let us walk, indeed.
You walk and day dream.
I walk and dip my nose into the belly
of the world. I find the markings my kind
leave in lieu of your history,
my éclaircissement, so to growl."

Big Dog thinks, "uppity dog."
He wonders where Little Dog learned
"in lieu of" and "éclaircissement"
in this bourgeois town.
This is their conspiracy.
Big Dog and Little Dog walk, scratch,
sniff the dog days of their lives,
talk up la vida perra they live.

"Sit dog! Sit still!"
Big Dog struggles with the leash,
the red leash, to hook it
to the halter on Little Dog,
then to his own hand, the hooked fingers.
Little Dog squirms and barks.
"Yes, Big Dog, let's walk.
You and me hooked on that leash.
Little Dog and Big Dog as one.
I keep you close to the earth.
You won't wander off forever
into the dream time that flows
with a great surge up and down
the red leash. You walk and dream,
Big Dog. I'll walk and pant beside you."

Leashed together
like two planets rotating
around their common center of gravity,
Little Dog and Big Dog set out

for the evening walk.
Huge red Texas sun
drops into the west.
The summer heat hangs on.
Red glow on the red leash.

III. Dwarf Yaupon

Barely out the front door,
Big Dog contemplates
the border of dwarf yaupon
around the front porch. How it gives way
to Asian Jasmine, the lantana,
and the low wave of buffalo grass
Big Dog calls "the lawn." Freshly mowed,
it mimics a lawn to fool an innocent eye.

Big Dog marvels at the yaupon's spreading bramble,
recalls how he climbed the thick cottonwood.
Autumn filled the branches with tatones.
He gathered pockets full of the hard green seeds,
used them as missiles in the schoolyard wars.
Somewhere in the deep furrow behind Big Dog's eyes,
a young boy sits forever perched
on the forked branch of the cottonwood.
He looks up, knows he can never drown
In that deepest of blue seas, the New Mexican sky
shimmering in the Zia sun of his childhood.

Little Dog knows nothing of this. He pants,
drools on the porch. Thinks doggedly
of his Oklahoma birth, the mongrel days,
the nightmare rains, running into the home

of Big Dog's relatives. The quick trip
south to sun-blasted Texas.

Memory of wolf and of wolf time
holds Little Dog and Big Dog locked
in a gaze that makes them dog friends.
"Here's a bone, Little Dog. Un huesito."
The bone game distracts Little Dog
from the walk, from the limitation of paws,
from the absence of the hunt,
from the longing for a bitch.

IV. Tatone Wars

Big Dog is lost in the tatone wars
inside his head. He's in the cottonwood,
while below the clean smell of his mother
rises up through branches and memory.
She hangs the laundry. Mother is thin,
a graceful ballerina. She twirls the white sheets
onto the line. Big Dog watches from his
alamo perch. He hears the zap, the hiss.
She falls away from the clothes line.
Mama survives. The telephone company apologizes
for the live wire it hooked up to the clothesline.
Big Dog keeps a sharp eye on the world.
He knows it will suddenly fry you.

Loss is a whip urging Big Dog on.
"Let's go, Little Dog. Let's walk."
He takes the first step away from the house.
Little Dog drops his bone at the sound
Big Dog makes with his lips, mouth, the entire

voice machinery Little Dog cannot grasp.
The tone means "walk." In Little Dog's brain,
there beats the music of the hunt. That time
the ancestor dogs gathered, hunger
was the red leash, and the pack howled,
picked up the scent of running deer,
circled in on the stricken doe.
That great time in the blood red snow.

The leash tightens. Little Dog plunges
ahead. Big Dog knows nothing
of the pack moving through snowy forests.
The pack consists of city dogs for him.
Two legged slurp slurppers. The big-eyed
toothy optimists of his haltered world.
He bristles and growls la vida perra. A snarl
for the rush hour traffic. A bark of discontent
for America, for the whole huckster pie.
Perra la vida perra but for now Big Dog
wants only to go on his merciful walk.

V. The First Few Steps

All beginnings come from the impulse,
the music, the word, not the tool
as Marx thought. The voice, the visions,
the dancing feet come first, then the tool.

Big Dog thinks each walk an expedition
not just around the heart of Dogtown,
but a setting out on a sea of words.
Welcome to the Expedition. First reports
as it heads out to sea, the music of the waves.

Nothing on this walk to detract from the word dance,
the pyrotechnics of signs and symbols,
the endless interference patterns
canceling out each wave, each life.
It is like a war here. The dog wars
of our dog days.

Big Dog takes one more step,
translates sound and motion into words,
the graphic marks on the page. Not important
the words be digitalized, regurgitated
on a computer screen, the full crt treatment.
"You know what I mean, how the graphic marks
leap back to the world," he says to Little Dog.
Not important, he thinks, how Little Dog's tail
looks like a semi-colon, humble
between his legs. Big Dog concedes to himself
the semi-colon doesn't wag, looks like
the remains of an animal, tail separated
from the body, now a pawless, clawless dot
on the brittle page, a speck of dust.

Big dog takes another step and it is good.
In the Hemingway sense that it is good.
The day is hot. Little Dog's tongue hangs slack,
drips on the sidewalk. He frowns, worries
Big Dog will be lost in his dream
before the walk truly begins. It is good
to move one step at a time, to feel the sidewalk
and grass coming up through your toes,
through foreleg and hind, he thinks. It is good
to dig in and scurry on like the ancestor packs
he remembers through his paws.
He lifts his leg and waters the yaupon.
It is good and a good way for the walk to begin.
Little Dog has no wine to drink. If he did,

he would drink. It would be good.
In the Hemingway sense.

One step, two, they are into it.
Little Dog, eyes and nose to the ground,
stops and trembles at every smell.
Big Dog dreams his cosmic dream,
trips over the broken sidewalk,
always in danger of failing,
falling, he falls. Tries to find grace
in the uncertain motions of his world.

Little Dog licks the face of Big Dog.
His tongue says "Get up, Big Dog,
get up." Big Dog gasps in pain,
stumbles to his feet. "Good boy,"
says Little Dog with his eyes.
They stagger on, red with the twilight sun.
Little Dog looks back, over his shoulder,
neck turned, brown eyes rolled
to show the whites. He makes sure
Big Dog is held by the leash.

Big Dog moans, stays on his feet.
The ceremonial walk must go on and on.
Little Dog yaps. One step, two steps
barely register on the spinning planet,
the tug and pull of gravity and galaxies,
the red leash, the dream time,
the Texas sun.

Acknowledgments

The poems in the first section, "In The Taverna Ononas,"
first appeared in the online chapbook "In The Taverna
Ononas" (Santa Fe Poetry Broadside: No. 14, March, 2000).
Many of these poems have been slightly revised since then.
"There Are Four Wounds, Miguel" first appeared in the chap-
book *There Are Four Wounds, Miguel* (University of North
Texas Press: A Trilobite Poetry Chapbook, 1994). The
Spanish version of "Pásale" did not appear in this earlier edi-
tion. For this edition, the poems of the earlier edition have
been slightly revised and five new ones have been added. "At
Concordia Cemetery, El Paso" and an earlier version of
"Jammin' in a chile house" were published in *Frank, An
International Journal of Contemporary Writing and Art*
(Paris, France: Nos. 16/17, 1998). The poem "Hilbert's Hotel"
first appeared in *Willow Street* (Albuquerque: March, 2000,).
"Liberación" first appeared in *Foghorn* (Albuquerque:
March/April, 1996). "In My Violin Dream" was published in
Back Door (Albuquerque: April, 2000). Earlier versions of "In
the San Antonio Hotel" were published in *Southwest, A
Contemporary Anthology* (Albuquerque: Red Earth Press,
1977) and in my book *The Unicorn Poem & Flowers and Songs
of Sorrow* (Albuquerque: West End Press, 1992). All other
poems in this book are appearing for the first time in print.

A special word of thanks to my brother, the biologist
Michael Mares, who discovered the Golden Viscacha Rat, which
I have appropriated for my own purposes.

About The Author

A native of **Albuquerque**, New Mexico, E. A. "Tony" Mares and his wife, the writer Carolyn Meyer, now live and write there. Mares has published extensively in English and Spanish as a poet, translator, essayist, playwright, fiction writer, journalist and historian. His poetry and fiction have been published nationally and internationally in *Frank*, *Prairie Schooner*, *Blue Mesa Review*, *Solo*, *Blanco Movil*, *New Mexico Poetry Renaissance*, *La Confluencia*, *Ceremony of Brotherhood*, and many other publications. He is the author of *The Unicorn Poem* (San Marcos Press), *The Unicorn Poem & Flowers and Songs of Sorrow* (West End Press), and *There Are Four Wounds, Miguel* (University of North Texas Press).

One of Mares' plays, "Lola's Last Dance," was published in David Richard Jones' anthology *New Mexico Plays* (University of New Mexico Press, 1989). During the1970s and '80s, he toured his one act play, "I Returned and Saw Under the Sun: Padre Martínez of Taos" throughout the Southwest. The play was published under this title by the University of New Mexico Press in 1989.

After completing a doctorate in European history at the University of New Mexico in 1973, Mares taught history, Spanish, and American literature at Colorado College, the University of New Mexico, the University of Arkansas, New Mexico Highlands University, the University of North Texas, and elsewhere.

Currently, he is at work on a memoir about his role in the historical reinterpretation of Padre Antonio José Martinez of Taos, a collection of short stories, and a collaborative social science book with Tomás Atencio and Miguel Montiel that addresses significant Chicano issues. He tries to write and work on poems on a regular basis. He enjoys visiting his grown children, María, Vered, and Ernesto, and his grandchildren Lianna, Danielle, and Shannon Rebecca.

Colophon

The first edition of *With the Eyes of a Raptor*, by E. A. Mares, is printed on 70 pound non-acidic Arbor paper, containing fifty percent post-consumer recycled fiber, by Edwards Brothers, Inc. of Ann Arbor, Michigan. Titles have been set in Caslon Openface and Bernhard Modern typefaces. The text was set in a contemporary version of Classic Bodoni, originally designed by the 18th century Italian typographer and punchcutter, Giambattista Bodoni, press director for the Duke of Parma. *With the Eyes of a Raptor* was designed by Bryce Milligan. The cover illustration is by Vered Mares.

Wings Press was founded in 1975 by J. Whitebird and Joseph F. Lomax as "an informal association of artists and cultural mythologists dedicated to the preservation of the literature of the nation of Texas." The publisher/editor since 1995, Bryce Milligan is honored to carry on and expand that mission to include the finest in American writing.

Other recent and forthcoming literature from Wings Press

Way of Whiteness by Wendy Barker (2000)
Hook & Bloodline by Chip Dameron (2000)
Incognito: Journey of a Secret Jew by María Espinosa (2002)
Street of the Seven Angels by John Howard Griffin (2003)
Black Like Me by John Howard Griffin (2004)
Winter Poems from Eagle Pond by Donald Hall (1999)
Initiations in the Abyss by Jim Harter (2002)
Strong Box Heart by Sheila Sánchez Hatch (2000)
Patterns of Illusion by James Hoggard (2002)
This Side of Skin by Deborah Paredez (2002)
Fishlight: A Dream of Childhood by Cecile Pineda (2001)
The Love Queen of the Amazon by Cecile Pineda (2001)
Bardo99 by Cecile Pineda (2002)
Face by Cecile Pineda (2003)
Smolt by Nicole Pollentier (1999)
Garabato Poems by Virgil Suárez (1999)
Sonnets to Human Beings by Carmen Tafolla (1999)
Sonnets and Salsa by Carmen Tafolla (2001)
The Laughter of Doves by Frances Marie Treviño (2001)
Finding Peaches in the Desert by Pam Uschuk (2000)
One-Legged Dancer by Pam Uschuk (2002)
Vida by Alma Luz Villanueva (2002)

Anthologies:

Cantos al Sexto Sol: A Collection of Aztlanahuac Writing
(2002), Edited by Cecilio García-Camarillo,
Roberto Rodríguez and Patrisia Gonzales
*Falling From Grace in Texas: A Literary Response to the Demise
of Paradise* (2004), Edited by Rick Bass and Paul Christensen